MOUSE

Sandie Lee Books

The Mouse

The mouse (or mice, if there is more than one) is a small animal in the rodent family. There are many varieties of this common animal. Domesticated mice come in many colors and sizes. This includes the spiny mouse, zebra mouse and the fancy mouse. Mice have been used in laboratories and kept as pets for many years. Mice are also considered pests. They can do a lot of damage to a farmer's crop or if they get into your home. Let's discover more about this little rodent.

Where in the World?

Did you know the mouse can be found most anywhere? This rodent can even be found in parts of the Antarctica. The mouse will live in most habitats but is commonly found in fields and in forests. It lives on the ground and will hide under dense vegetation or fallen logs.

The Body of a Mouse

Did you know the mouse's tail is very long? The body of the mouse only measures about 1 to 7 inches long. Its tail, however, can be longer than its body. The mouse has short hair that comes in a variety of colors. It has a pointed nose, small round ears and black beady eyes.

The Senses of a Mouse

Did you know the mouse has poor eyesight? Even though the mouse's eyes are very predominate on its face, it lacks great eyesight. The mouse relies on its keen hearing and good sense of smell to avoid predators and to search out food. The feet on the mouse also enable it to run backwards.

What a Mouse Eats

Did you know the mouse is mostly a herbivore? This means the mouse eats mostly plant matter and grains. Even though the mouse is known for loving cheese, this is not something it encounters in the wild. The front teeth of the mouse are very long and sharp. They are perfect for gnawing through tough objects.

The Feet of a Mouse

Did you know the mouse has soft feet? Each foot on the mouse has soft pads on the bottom and sharp nails on each two - this makes it a great climber. The mouse has 4 toes on its front feet and 5 toes on its back ones. A mouse uses its front feet to grip its food.

The Mouse's Special Ability

Did you know the mouse is an excellent swimmer? A mouse can swim and even stay under the water for several minutes. Some species of the mouse can also jump really high - nearly 18 inches into the air. Since the mouse is so small it has to be able to get away from predators quickly.

The Mouse as Prey

Did you know mice are eaten by many different species? Various animals and birds hunt mice. Predatory animals like the fox, cats, dogs and coyotes will all catch and eat mice. Birds like the hawk and eagle will also dine on mice. Snakes of various sizes catch mice and swallow them whole.

Mouse Talk

Did you know the mouse can make sounds? A mouse will make many noises, some we can hear and others we cannot. A mouse will typically make squeaking sounds. When a mouse is in your house, you can sometimes hear it making scratching and chewing sounds. A mouse will also grind its teeth, but it may be too quiet for us to hear.

Mom Mouse

Did you know a mother mouse can have many litters of babies throughout her lifetime? A female mouse can become pregnant when she is very young. She will carry her young for less than a month. Her litter size can contain as many as 10 baby mice. In the wild, she will find a safe, warm place to have her babies.

Baby Mice

Did you know baby mice are born without hair? Baby mice are called, pups. They are born very tiny, hairless, blind, deaf and totally helpless. Within 5 to 7 days their hair will start to grow and their ears can hear. By 2 weeks of age, the eyes will be open and they will be walking around.

Mice as Pets

Did you know the common mouse is often kept as a pet? A mouse can make a great pet. It is very gentle and very active. To keep a mouse as a pet, you will need a cage, some bedding for the bottom, a water bottle and a food dish.

Life of a Mouse

Did you know mice have a very short lifespan in the wild? Since mice are hunted by a lot of different animals, most don't live very long. However, in captivity, a pet mouse can live to be around 2 years-old. Some mice are bred specifically to feed pet snakes.

The Deer Mouse

This species of mouse is found all over North America. It will live in the forest, prairies and desert regions. It can be brown to grey in color. It has white feet and a white underbelly. The whiskers and tail of this species are very long. It can grow to be about 3.5 inches long (not including its tail).

The African Pygmy Mouse

This little guy is the smallest mouse on the planet. It only measures from 1.2 to 3.1 inches long. The African pygmy mouse will stack small pebbles in front of its home. Once the dew collects on the rocks, the mouse laps it up. These mice are highly social and need to be with other mice.

Quiz

Question 1: What part of the mouse's body can be twice the length of its body?

Answer 1: Its tail

Question 2: What special ability does the mouse have?

Answer 2: It can run backwards

Question 3: How many baby mice can a mother mouse have at one time?

Answer 3: Around 10

Question 4: If you keep a mouse as a pet, what will it drink its water from?

Answer 4: A water bottle

Question 5: What is the smallest mouse species?

Answer 5: The African pygmy mouse

Thank you for checking out another addition from Sandie Lee Books! Make sure to check out Amazon.com for many other great titles.

www.ingramcontent.com/pod-product-compliance
Lightning Source LLC
Chambersburg PA
CBHW040328010626
45792CB00024B/2289